Today's Superstars

Entertainment

Beyoncé

by Geoffrey M. Horn

GARETH**STEVENS**
GS
PUBLISHING

A Member of the WRC Media Family of Companies

Please visit our web site at: www.garethstevens.com
For a free color catalog describing Gareth Stevens Publishing's
list of high-quality books and multimedia programs, call
1-800-542-2595 (USA) or 1-800-387-3178 (Canada).
Gareth Stevens Publishing's fax: (414) 332-3567.

Library of Congress Cataloging-in-Publication Data

Horn, Geoffrey M.
    Beyoncé / by Geoffrey M. Horn.
      p. cm. — (Today's superstars. Entertainment)
    Includes bibliographical references and index.
    ISBN 0-8368-4230-8 (lib. bdg.)
    1. Knowles, Beyoncé—Juvenile literature. 2. Singers—United
States—Biography—Juvenile literature. I. Title.
ML3930.K66H67   2005
782.42164'092—dc22
    [B]   2005049944

This edition first published in 2006 by
Gareth Stevens Publishing
A Member of the WRC Media Family of Companies
330 West Olive Street, Suite 100
Milwaukee, WI 53212 USA

This edition copyright © 2006 by Gareth Stevens, Inc.

Editor: Jim Mezzanotte
Art direction and design: Tammy West
Picture research: Diane Laska-Swanke

Photo credits: Cover, p. 9 © Frank Micelotta/Getty Images; p. 5 © Carlos
Alvarez/Getty Images; p. 7 © Dana Nalbandian/WireImage.com; pp. 12, 18,
27 Photofest; p. 14 © Dave Rossman/WireImage.com; p. 17 © Marion Curtis/
DMI/Time & Life Pictures/Getty Images; p. 21 © Vaughn Youtz/Getty Images;
p. 23 © Jim Smeal/WireImage.com; p. 28 © Carlo Allegri/Getty Images

Printed in the United States of America

1 2 3 4 5 6 7 8 9 08 07 06 05

Contents

Chapter 1

The Diva Next Door

From the moment Beyoncé walks on stage, you can see she is a diva (DEE-vah). Just don't call her one to her face. "I've never thought I was better than anybody else," she writes. "And I have to live my life trying to prove that to people. I can't win. Critics want to make me out to be a diva control freak … It's very irritating."

Divas have their own way of walking and talking, their own sense of style. Some divas get bad press — often with good reason. They're very talented. But they are often very demanding, too. They love the spotlight, and they're not always willing to share it.

Kelly Rowland has sung with Beyoncé in the group Destiny's Child. She knows something about being a diva. She says

The Italian Connection

"Diva" comes from an old Latin word that means goddess. It has the same root as the English word "divine." The first singers to be called divas were opera stars in Italy. Divas were women who sang like goddesses — and wanted others to treat them that way.

Beyoncé strikes a diva-like pose while making an appearance for Pepsi in Madrid, Spain.

5

you need to show "a little bit of cockiness when you're on that stage." She thinks the group members knew how to stop being divas when the show ended. "Because when you take that attitude offstage, it becomes a problem. You start feeling like it's all about you, but it's not."

Beyoncé is a different kind of diva. *Entertainment Weekly* called her the "diva next door." She is a pop superstar. But she wants people to know that success hasn't spoiled her or made her stuck-up. "Sometimes I think, 'What if I get too famous?'" she told a reporter for *Essence*. "I want to go to the store or go to a mall … and not worry about being recognized."

From Diana to Destiny
Diana Ross was one of the first pop stars to be called a diva. She sang with the Supremes. In the 1960s, they were the world's most popular female group. They first sang together as teenagers in Detroit. At first, Florence Ballard was the group leader. But when the Supremes started making hits, Diana Ross got the juicy lead parts.

Hip-Hop Meets Opera

Is Beyoncé a diva? Some people at MTV must think so. The network picked her to star in a hip-hop version of the classical opera *Carmen*. This made-for-TV movie aired in 2001. In it, Beyoncé plays Carmen, a woman who treats other people badly. But she is very beautiful, and no man can resist her. It's a classic diva part. Beyoncé was only eighteen when she shot the film. But even then, she had the voice, moves, and beauty to carry it off.

Diana Ross was still very much a diva when this photo was taken in 1991.

Fact File

Diana Ross had twelve number-one pop singles with the Supremes. She had six more number-one singles after she became a superstar on her own.

Fame took its toll. Soon, the Supremes became known as Diana Ross and the Supremes. Then the group broke up. In the 1970s, Diana Ross went solo. She had hit records. She starred in movies and on TV. She played the top clubs in to-die-for outfits.

"She was gorgeous … and she had that big, beautiful hair," Antonio "L.A." Reid wrote in *Rolling Stone*. "And, of course, she was glamorous. I remember all those furs, diamonds and early bling-bling. Everything about her — her mannerisms, her look, her aura — exuded stardom."

You could say much the same about Beyoncé. Right now, her voice, face, and figure are almost everywhere you turn. Like Diana Ross, Beyoncé has sold millions of records, both as part of a group and on her own. As an actress, she has starred in several movies. She's sung on major awards shows. She's performed at the Super Bowl and for President George W. Bush. She's signed big advertising deals with Pepsi and L'Oreal. She's putting

Fact File

Beyoncé performed with Destiny's Child on a VH1 special, "Divas 2000: A Tribute to Diana Ross." Donna Summer and Mariah Carey were also on the program.

out her own line of clothing, jewelry, and perfume. Divas don't get much hotter.

Beyoncé understands the dangers of being a diva. She sounds sincere when she says she wants to share the spotlight. Beyoncé knows that when Destiny's Child sang on TV, the cameras mostly focused on her. She says she often told the TV people, "Please, please give the other girls equal time. This is not the Supremes."

Destiny's Child in Tokyo, Japan, in April 2005. Two months later, the group announced plans to split up when its "Destiny Fulfilled" tour ended. From left to right: Beyoncé, Michelle Williams, and Kelly Rowland.

Chapter 2

Workin' It

Beyoncé comes from a hard-working, well-off family. Her parents are Tina and Matthew Knowles. They met in Houston in the mid-1970s. At the time, Tina worked at a bank, and Matthew had a job with a big company. They were married in 1981. Tina gave birth to their first child, Beyoncé Giselle Knowles, on September 4, 1981. Five years later, Beyoncé's sister Solange was born.

Soul Survivors is a book about Destiny's Child. The group members tell their own stories. In the book, Beyoncé discusses her childhood. She writes, "I grew up watching my mom and dad work their butts off — and I learned a lot from them." Beyoncé's father earned a big income selling medical equipment. Her mother saved enough money to open her own hair salon. "We are very focused," Matthew later told *Ebony*. "We know what our goals are. We show up and we suit up. We do whatever it takes to get the job done."

Something Special

Beyoncé was shy when she was very young. Her parents didn't push her. They didn't think of her as a future superstar. When Beyoncé was seven, she began taking a dance class. Her dance teacher thought she had something special. The teacher urged Beyoncé to sing at a school talent show. Beyoncé sang "Imagine," a song by John Lennon.

When Beyoncé's parents saw her at the talent show, they were amazed. On stage, their shy little girl didn't seem so shy any more. "I felt at home on that stage, more so than anywhere else," she writes. Even at age seven, she knew how to work a crowd.

Fact File

John Lennon wrote "Imagine" in 1971, after he left the Beatles. Beyoncé says it's still one of her favorite songs.

Kelly's Destiny

Kelly Rowland's birth name is Kelendria. She was born in Atlanta, Georgia, on February 11, 1981. Kelly did not see her father much while she was growing up. She moved with her mother to Houston in 1990. Money was a big problem for the Rowland family. Kelly's mom worked as a live-in nanny, moving from house to house. Kelly did not have a very stable home life.

When Kelly joined Beyoncé in Girls Tyme, the two became friends. The Knowles family offered to let Kelly live with them. Her mom agreed. "I was lucky," Kelly writes in *Soul Survivors*. "Sharing a room with Beyoncé was like a slumber party every night, but much louder." Kelly and Beyoncé are the only members of Destiny's Child who appear on all the group's albums. Kelly had success with a 2002 solo album, *Simply Deep*.

Kelly Rowland in 2001.

Winning and Losing

Beyoncé's parents urged her to enter more contests. In these contests, girls were judged on beauty as well as talent. Beyoncé felt awkward about the beauty part. But she loved the singing and dancing. Within a few years, her bedroom was full of trophies for first place.

By 1990, Beyoncé was performing with a local group called Girls Tyme. All the group members were eight or nine years old. Beyoncé was the lead vocalist. Kelly Rowland joined the group as a singer in 1991. Kelly and Beyoncé became close friends. That year, Kelly moved in with the Knowles family.

Girls Tyme sang and danced to pop and R&B tunes. The girls learned some of their moves from watching videos of pop groups. They watched groups such as the Jackson Five and the Supremes. Tina Knowles styled all the girls' hair. They showed off their steps to the customers at her beauty shop.

By 1992, the girls were ready for their big break. After months and months of rehearsing, they got on the TV show *Star Search*. They made it all the way to the finals — and then lost. Beyoncé remembers the moment they got the bad news: "We bit back our tears and wore like the fakest smiles on our lips." Only when the cameras stopped rolling did the girls run offstage and let the tears flow.

That night, the members of Girls Tyme cried themselves to sleep. They were sure their singing careers were over.

Beyoncé's father and mother, Matthew and Tina Knowles.

Taking Control

When Beyoncé was a little girl, Tina and Matthew Knowles tried hard not to be pushy parents. After Girls Tyme lost on *Star Search*, their attitude was different. Matthew thought Beyoncé could become a superstar. He decided to do everything he could to make it happen.

Matthew gave up his high-paying job to manage his daughter's career. Tina kept the hair salon. She had to work harder than ever to support the family. Their marriage was in deep trouble.

"It was very stressful," Tina says. "We went from having two really great incomes to having one. We had to scale down the house. Sell the cars. It was a really tough time for us.… I felt like he was a little too driven." Tina and Matthew separated for a while but then got back together.

Searching for Success

For years, Matthew struggled to make his daughter a star. The first step was creating the right group. Beyoncé was the key building block. Next came her friend Kelly Rowland, who was already living with the Knowles family. Then, LaTavia Roberson joined the group. She had been a dancer with Girls Tyme. LeToya Luckett was another Houston girl. She became the fourth member of the group.

The girls had a rough time landing a record contract. Columbia Records agreed to give them a tryout. But the girls went swimming the night before. Their noses were stuffy, and they didn't sing too well. Then, in 1995, they thought they had a deal with Elektra Records. But the label dropped them a few months later.

During this time, Matthew and the girls kept tinkering with the group's name.

Fact File

Tina's beauty shop is called Headliners. It is still one of Houston's best. But Tina no longer cuts hair there. She spends most of her time working on Beyoncé's career.

16

The Motown Model

Matthew Knowles had a business degree from college. He was also a great salesman. But he knew little about the music industry. To learn more, he studied the career of Berry Gordy. Gordy was the man behind Motown. He started Motown in Detroit in the late 1950s. At first, it was a tiny record company. By the 1970s, it was a huge, successful business. Gordy guided Diana Ross and the Supremes, the Jackson Five, and many others.

Gordy had a sharp eye for talent. But he also thought a record firm should do more than just crank out records. Motown worked hard to turn talented young singers into superstars. Gordy hired coaches who taught them how to walk, talk, and dress. He had the last word on every major decision. Matthew followed the same plan when building Destiny's Child.

Destiny's Child was a foursome when the group made this 1998 appearance. From left to right: LaTavia, Beyoncé, LeToya, and Kelly.

A Matter of Faith

Beyoncé's faith in God is very important to her. In 2003, she told the *Washington Post*, "The thing that keeps me centered and grounded is knowing that I'm always protected and that God is in control of certain things." Even the name Destiny's Child reminds Beyoncé of her faith. "Destiny represents God," she said. The group added "child" because "we feel like we're children of God's."

Beyoncé in a church scene from her 2003 film *The Fighting Temptations*.

After Girls Tyme they were Somethin' Fresh. Then they were Borderline — for about a week. The name Cliché got old fast. So did their next choice, the Dolls. Tina favored Destiny, a word she spotted when she opened a Bible. But that name was already taken. Finally, they settled on Destiny's Child — and struck gold.

One Last Chance

In 1997, Columbia flew the girls to New York for another tryout. "We knew it might be our last chance, so we couldn't mess it up," Beyoncé writes in *Soul Survivors*. They thought the date went well. But they didn't know for sure.

Beyoncé learned the good news at her mother's beauty shop several weeks later. "We started screaming and crying right in the middle of the salon. The ladies with their heads under the dryers looked at us like we were crazy."

Fact File

Destiny's Child sang "Killing Time" on the *Men in Black* movie soundtrack album in 1997. Another budding superstar had a single on that same album: Alicia Keys.

Chapter 4

And Then There Were Three

The girls' first album, *Destiny's Child*, came out in February 1998. Beyoncé was sixteen years old, and Kelly had just turned seventeen. The album sold more than a half million copies. These sales weren't great. But they were good enough to earn the group a second shot.

The album offers a lesson in how to mix a hit record. "No, No, No" shows up twice on *Destiny's Child*. Part 1 has a singsong sound that often feels as simple as a nursery rhyme. Part 2 is the big hit. It is a remix by Wyclef Jean. He works magic with the tune, layering the girls' voices over a hip-hop beat. It sounds much more grown-up.

Fact File

Rapping near the end of "No, No, No," Wyclef Jean sums up the history of Destiny's Child: "They went from a dream to the young Supremes. Sing it, girls!"

Chart-topping TLC

In the 1990s, Destiny's Child wasn't the only all-female group making R&B hits. Another top-selling girl group was TLC, based in Atlanta. TLC formed in 1991. The group's three members were Tionne "T-Boz" Watkins, Lisa "Left-Eye" Lopes, and Rozonda "Chilli" Thomas. They scored a huge success in 1994 with the album *CrazySexyCool*. They rocked the charts again in 1999 with *Fanmail* and the single "No Scrubs." Tragedy struck TLC in 2002 when Left-Eye was killed in a car crash. Chilli made news two years later when she broke up with R&B superstar Usher.

TLC in concert in Anaheim, California, in 2000.

The song is faster, tighter, shorter, and sharper — an R&B radio smash.

The next Destiny's Child album, *The Writing's on the Wall*, hit stores in July 1999. The first single, "Bills, Bills, Bills," was an instant hit. "Say My Name" was an even bigger sensation. It won two Grammy Awards, Best R&B Song and Best R&B Performance by a Group. The album went on to sell more than ten million copies. Destiny's Child was exploding — in more ways than one.

Survivors

Tensions had been building for years. Beyoncé and Kelly were good friends. They were also close with Matthew and Tina Knowles. But LaTavia and LeToya felt like outsiders. They were unhappy with the way Matthew ran the group. In December 1999, they told Matthew they wanted to choose their own managers.

Matthew moved quickly. Within weeks, LaTavia and LeToya were out of the group. Michelle Williams and Farrah Franklin were in.

Michelle's Destiny

Michelle's full name is Tenetria Michelle Williams.
She was born in Rockford, Illinois, on July 23, 1980. She
sang in church and at school when she was growing up.
But she didn't think of music as a career until she got to
college. Michelle was a backup singer for teen R&B star
Monica before she joined Destiny's Child. She went solo
on the pop-gospel albums *Heart to Yours* (2002) and *Do
You Know* (2004).

By March 2000, Destiny's Child
had two new members, Michelle and
Farrah, along with Kelly and Beyoncé.

Destiny's Child was still a foursome, but not for long. Farrah never really bonded with Beyoncé and Kelly. She couldn't take the group's crazy pace. She missed rehearsals. She didn't want to tour. By July 2000, Farrah was gone.

When *Survivor* came out in May 2001, the group was down to three members: Beyoncé, Kelly, and Michelle. Kelly shared many of the lead vocals. But Beyoncé had the major role in the studio. She co-wrote and co-produced nearly every song on the album.

Survivor opens with "Independent Women Part I." It was already a hit from the *Charlie's Angels* movie soundtrack a year earlier. But the tightest and most talked-about track on the album was "Bootylicious." "I wrote that song because I was getting bigger and bigger," Beyoncé told *Newsweek* magazine. "I like to eat. That's a problem in this industry. I'm still probably twice as big as any of the other actresses out there."

Foxxy

For Beyoncé, Kelly, and Michelle, 2001 was a year of Destiny. In January, Destiny's Child performed at George W. Bush's inauguration as U.S. president. "Bootylicious" ruled the pop charts in August. In December, *Billboard* magazine named the group Artist of the Year for the second year in a row.

Even as the honors rolled in, there were signs the band had peaked. All three members were working on solo projects. Destiny's Child wasn't ready to break up — not yet. But hype about the group had cooled. The hot news was all Beyoncé, Beyoncé, Beyoncé.

In 2002, Beyoncé made her big-screen debut. She starred in the movie *Austin Powers in Goldmember*. Beyoncé plays Foxxy Cleopatra. Wearing an Afro wig and hip-hugger pants, she looks like she stepped right out of the early 1970s.

Fewer people saw Beyoncé's next movie, *The Fighting Temptations*. In this 2003 drama, she plays a singer who's also a single mom. The film's best parts are the musical numbers, in which Beyoncé sings soul and R&B as well as gospel.

A Diva Goes Solo

Beyoncé made her solo album break-through in 2003 with *Dangerously in Love*. The album was a huge success. Many critics thought she sang better as a solo diva than as part of a group. Two standout cuts were "Crazy in Love," with Jay-Z, and "Baby Boy," with Sean Paul. You couldn't get these tunes out of your head. They were matched to sizzling dance videos.

The buzz centered on "Crazy in Love." Rumor had it that there was a romance between Beyoncé and Jay-Z. Beyoncé kept her feelings private.

But Jay-Z's friends were sure. "I've never seen him sprung like this," one source told *Rolling Stone* magazine. "He cares about her, gives her great advice…. They adore each other."

Beyoncé isn't shy about praising Jay-Z for his help with *Dangerously in Love.* "I'm amazed how much he knows about how much," she says. "He can write a song for a woman. He can write a song for anybody." For "Crazy in Love," he came to the studio at 2:00 A.M. He wrote the rap in his head in about ten minutes.

Fact File

Dangerously in Love earned Beyoncé five Grammy Awards, including Best R&B Song for "Crazy in Love." She also won four *Billboard* Music Awards in 2003.

Despite her solo success, Beyoncé did not forget Destiny's Child. In 2004, the group returned to the studio for *Destiny Fulfilled*. In early 2005, the group launched a world tour to promote the new album.

Members of the group insisted they wanted to keep performing and recording together. By June 2005, however, they were singing a different tune. They announced that Destiny's Child would split up when the tour was over. "Now is the time to pursue our personal goals and solo efforts," they said. The move left Beyoncé free to pursue her own destiny as a solo diva.

Time Line

1981	Beyoncé Giselle Knowles is born September 4 in Houston, Texas.
1991	Kelly Rowland joins Beyoncé in Girls Tyme and moves in with the Knowles family.
1992	Girls Tyme loses in the finals on *Star Search*.
1998	*Destiny's Child* is released.
2000	"Say My Name" becomes a number-one pop hit. After several changes in membership, Destiny's Child goes from a foursome to a trio.
2001	*Survivor* is released. "Bootylicious" becomes a hit single.
2002	Beyoncé plays Foxxy Cleopatra in *Austin Powers in Goldmember*.
2003	Her solo album *Dangerously in Love* features "Crazy in Love" with Jay-Z.
2004	The group releases *Destiny Fulfilled*.
2005	Destiny's Child announces group's breakup.

Glossary

charts — in the music business, lists of the most popular, best-selling artists.

diva — a successful and glamorous female singer.

exuded — showed a certain quality in a strong way.

gospel — a form of Christian religious music.

Grammy — an award given out by by people who work in the music business.

inauguration — an event that marks the start of something, such as a term in office.

lyrics — the words to a song.

mix — in music, to put together all the layers of sound that are recorded for a song.

opera — a drama with singing and other music.

R&B — short for rhythm and blues. At first, R&B was a mix of blues and dance rhythms. Today, it includes many kinds of African American pop music.

slang — words used on the street or in casual writing but not normally used in formal writing.

soul — in music, a mix of R&B and gospel that first became popular in the 1950s.

vocalist — singer.

To Find Out More

Books

Beyoncé. Blue Banner Biographies (series).
Kathleen Tracy (Mitchell Lane)

Beyoncé Knowles. Star Files (series).
Nicola Hodgson (Raintree)

The History of Motown. African American Achievers
(series). Virginia Aronson (Chelsea House)

Videos

Austin Powers in Goldmember (New Line) PG-13

Beyoncé: Live at Wembley (Sony) NR

The Fighting Temptations (Paramount) PG-13

Web Sites

Beyoncé
www.beyonceonline.com
Beyoncé's own official site

Destiny's Child
www.destinyschild.com
The official site of Destiny's Child

Index

About the Author

Geoffrey M. Horn has been a fan of music, movies, and sports for as long as he can remember. He has written more than a dozen books for young people and adults, along with hundreds of articles on many different subjects. He lives in southwestern Virginia, in the foothills of the Blue Ridge Mountains, with his wife, their collie, and four cats. He dedicates this book to anyone who wants to be a star — and is willing to work hard enough to get there.